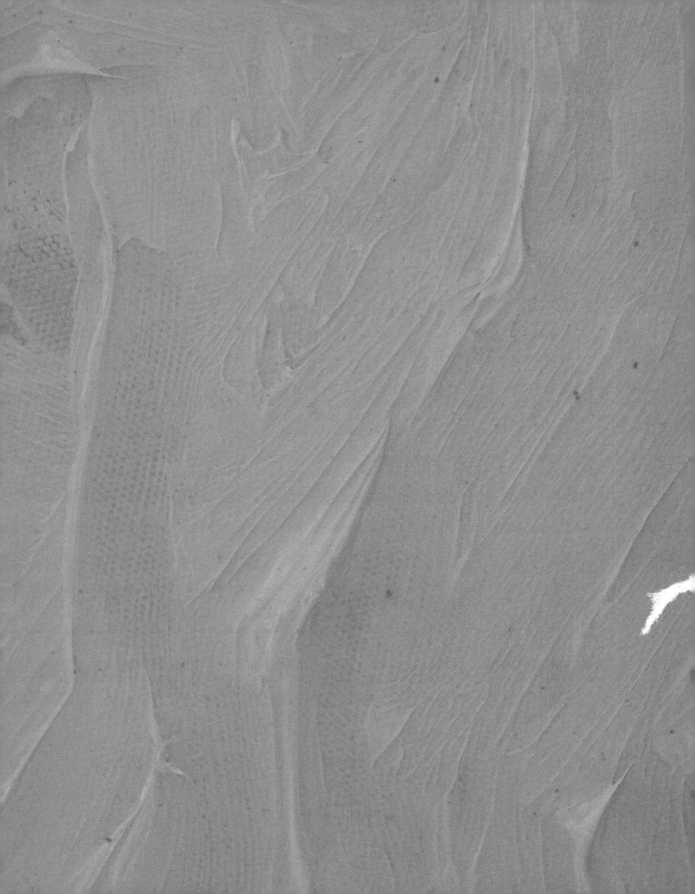

Brush with Greatness

REMBRANDT VAN RIJN

Amie Jane Leavitt

CURIOUS FOX BOOKS™

© 2025 by Curious Fox Books™, an imprint of Fox Chapel Publishing Company, Inc.

Brush with Greatness: Rembrandt van Rijn is a revision of *Rembrandt*, published in 2017 by Purple Toad Publishing, Inc. Reproduction of its contents is strictly prohibited without written permission from the rights holder.

Paperback ISBN 979-8-89094-164-0
Hardcover ISBN 979-8-89094-165-7

Library of Congress Control Number: 2024949113

To learn more about the other great books from Fox Chapel Publishing, or to find a retailer near you, call toll-free 800-457-9112, send mail to 903 Square Street, Mount Joy, PA 17552, or visit us at *www.FoxChapelPublishing.com*.

We are always looking for talented authors. To submit an idea, please send a brief inquiry to acquisitions@foxchapelpublishing.com.

Fox Chapel Publishing makes every effort to use environmentally friendly paper for printing.

Printed in China

Contents

Christ in the Storm on the Sea of Galilee shows drama on the sea and on the men's faces.

CHAPTER 1

Windmills, Canals, and Artists

Last night I dreamed about a painting I saw in art class. In the painting, a stormy sea tosses a tall ship to and fro. The sailors try to keep the ship from flipping over.

I felt like I could swim right up to the ship and climb aboard. I could almost hear the crashing waves and smell the salty sea. The painting seemed so real, I even felt seasick.

All the way home, I couldn't stop thinking about the painting. And then it followed me into my dreams. The artist, Rembrandt (**REHM-brant**), has painted many powerful works of

The Mill is dark at the edges, making the bright center stand out.

art. He is also my teacher. I sure am lucky to be learning from this talented man!

I couldn't wait to get to art class today. I walked quickly along the brick lane. A windmill stands tall down the street, which is common to see in Holland. Its blades spin in slow circles when the wind blows. Small boats float in the canal along the road. House lights sparkle on the water, twinkling like stars in the sky. Amsterdam is such a pretty place. No wonder such a famous artist lives here.

"Good morning, Mariska **(mahr-ISH-kah)**!" Rembrandt greets me as I walk into his studio. "You are here early today!" He is standing near his easel, which holds his latest masterpiece.

The Artist in His Studio shows Rembrandt about to work on a new painting.

"What do you call this one?" I ask as I walk closer to the canvas.

Rembrandt chuckles. "Can't you tell who this is?" He stands next to the painting, smiling.

"Of course, teacher! It is you! You are doing another self-portrait!"

"Yes, another one. I must've done 40 self-portraits. But people like them, so I do them," he explains. He puts his paintbrush on the table and walks toward the door. The other students have just arrived.

"Let's take a field trip, students!" he says. "Follow me."

Self-portraits (shown here) and portraits are some of Rembrandt's most famous works.

Groningen

⊛ AMSTERDAM

• Leiden
NETHERLANDS
(HOLLAND)

Germany

Belgium

Rembrandt's home and
studio in Amsterdam
is now a museum for
the artist.

CHAPTER 2

A Painter of Light

As we walk along the canal, Rembrandt tells us stories about his life as an artist. He grew up in Leiden **(LIY-dihn)**, a town south of Amsterdam **(AM-ster-dam)**. His father owned a windmill on the Rhine **(RIYN)** River.

Rembrandt was the youngest of 10 children, but he still got to go to school. "I went to Latin school as a boy," he tells us now. "I learned a lot about the Bible and other important books there."

I picture some of his art in my mind. "Is this why you often paint Bible stories?"

"Yes, child," Rembrandt replies.

"I like your Bible paintings," my classmate Levi says. "My favorite is *The Parable* **(PAYR-uh-bul)** *of the Rich Fool*. The candle in the painting lights up everything that is important to the man. The way you painted it makes it look like a real light is shining on the painting. How do you do that?"

"Painting light isn't easy, Levi, but I will show you how to do it. I learned from my first art teacher, Jacob van Swanenburgh **(SWAYN-ehn-berg)**. He was a master painter of fire."

Rembrandt points to the canal. "Look at the way the sunlight flickers. It looks like a golden torch is in the water. Notice where you see light. Think about its color. Then you will know how to add it to your paintings."

Rembradt's father may have been the model for *The Parable of the Rich Fool.*

The Night Watch was even larger when Rembrandt made it, but it was later trimmed to fit a new location.

CHAPTER 3

Watching the Night

We stroll to the end of the street. Rembrandt opens the door to the Musketeer **(muhs-keh-TEER)** Meeting Hall. Several men tip their hats to greet us as we follow our teacher inside.

Rembrandt points to a huge painting in the grand hall. It stretches 12 feet (3.7 meters) across and more than 14 feet (4.3 meters) high. "This is my largest painting. It took me three years to finish," he explains. "People call it *The Night Watch* because of the dark colors."

I can tell it is Rembrandt's artwork because of the light in the painting. He painted two men talking to each

Jonah and the Whale by Pieter Lastman, Rembrandt's teacher, shows a scene from the Bible.

other. The sun is shining just on them. The other people in the painting are more in the shadows. One man in the corner holds a drum. Others are loading their muskets. It is clear that the men are getting ready for some kind of battle. There is a woman in the painting, too. I wonder where they are all going or what they are doing. Then I see a dog! I could stare at this painting for days and never see everything!

"I learned how to paint history like this from my second teacher," Rembrandt explains. "His name was Pieter Lastman **(PEE-ter LAST-man)**. He is the reason I moved to Amsterdam. Good teachers are very important for artists," he says with a smile.

The Good Samaritan at the Inn is a Rembrandt etching based on one of his paintings.

CHAPTER 4

More Than One Kind of Art

When we get back to the studio, Rembrandt asks, "Do artists only do one kind of art?"

"Some do, some don't," answers another student. "Which type are you, teacher?"

"You know that I paint," he says. "But did you know that I do etchings, too?"

I look around the room. All of my classmates have the same blank look I have. "What is an etching?" I finally ask.

"I'm so glad you asked, Mariska!" Rembrandt claps his hands with delight. "We will have our first lesson right now!"

(Left) The plate on which Rembrandt etched *Abraham Entertaining the Angels*. (Right) The print made from the etching.

Rembrandt opens a drawer and pulls out a pile of paper. They have pictures on them, made with black ink. "I didn't draw these on the paper," he explains. "I drew them on a metal plate covered in a type of wax. To make an etching, I use a needle to scrape a picture into the wax. Then I dip the plate in a special liquid. When I am done, I can use the metal plate to print many copies of my drawing."

The *Hundred Guilder Print* was famous in its day, costing this amount to buy. "Guilder" was the money used in the Netherlands.

As I listen, I feel like a flame is lit in my mind. What a brilliant idea! With an etching, you can have many copies of a picture, not just one. I say, "This is like the way our printing press makes our books!"

"It is very similar!" Rembrandt says, smiling. "Etchings are a special form of art that allows it to be shared with more people."

When the clock strikes six, class ends for the day. I hurry out the door to make my way home. I am so excited about all I have learned today. I can't wait to tell my parents about it.

The Sampling Officials almost looks down on viewers, showing the men's importance.

CHAPTER 5

An Artist's Life

When I fall asleep, my dreams are sweet. I don't dream of sailing ships and rolling seas like I did last night. Instead I dream of kind musketeers tipping their hats. And I dream of learning more about art from the famous Rembrandt. I can't wait to find out what we will learn tomorrow.

In the years that come, Rembrandt's style will become so loved by his students that thousands of works will be linked to him. He didn't make that many, but he did create hundreds of paintings and etchings. The beauty of Rembrandt's work will continue to shine for years to come.

1606	Rembrant Harmenszoon van Rijn **(REHM-brant HAR-men-sun van REHN)** is born on July 15.
1620–1623	Rembrandt studies with Jacob van Swanenburgh.
1624	Rembrandt spends six months studying with Pieter Lastman in Amsterdam, then sets up a studio in Leiden.
1628	Rembrandt begins teaching art to his first students. He begins etching.
1631	Rembrandt moves to Amsterdam permanently. He focuses on portraits, which make him famous.
1633	Rembrandt adds the silent *D* to his name.
1634	Rembrandt marries Saskia van Uylenburgh **(SASS-kiah van OO-len-berg)**. She is the model for many of his paintings.
1639	The family moves to a house in Amsterdam that becomes known as Rembrandt House.
1642	Saskia dies.
1649	Rembrandt meets his future wife, Hendrickje Stoffels **(HEN-reek-ee STOHF-els)**. She becomes a model for him as well.
1655	Rembrandt declares bankruptcy. His money problems continue the rest of his life.
1669	Rembrandt dies on October 4.

Paintings

1624	*The Three Singers*
1628	*Artist in His Studio*
1630	*David Playing the Harp for King Saul*
1631	*Portrait of Nicolaes Ruts*
1632	*The Anatomy Lesson of Dr. Nicolaes Tulp*
1633	*The Storm on the Sea of Galilee*
1635–1638	*Belshazzar's Feast*
1642	*The Night Watch*
1654	*Bathsheba at Her Bath*
1655	*The Polish Rider*
1660	*The Return of the Prodigal Son*
1660	*Self-Portrait with Two Circles*
1662	*The Sampling Officials*
1667	*The Jewish Bride*

Etchings

1633	*Joseph's Coat Brought to Jacob*
1633	*The Good Samaritan at the Inn*
1638	*The Little Jewish Bride*
1640	*Sleeping Puppy*
1640	*View of Amsterdam from the Northwest*
1647–1649	*Hundred Guilder Print*
1651	*The Flight Into Egypt: A Night Piece*
1652	*David in Prayer*
1652	*Christ Preaching*
1655	*The Goldsmith*

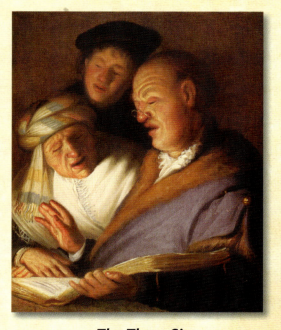

The Three Singers shows warmth and light, like most Rembrandt paintings.

Works Consulted

Dickey, Stephanie. "Rembrandt at 400." *Smithsonian Magazine*. December 2006. Retrieved July 15, 2016. http://www.smithsonianmag.com/arts-culture/rembrandt-at-400-138954962/

"Rembrandt, 1606–1669." *National Gallery*. Retrieved July 15, 2016. https://www.nationalgallery.org.uk/artists/rembrandt

"Rembrandt van Rijn (1606–1669): Paintings." *The Met*. Retrieved July 15, 2016. http://www.metmuseum.org/toah/hd/rmbt/hd_rmbt.htm

Wetering, E. van de. "Rembrandt." *Encyclopedia Britannica*. Retrieved July 15, 2016. https://www.britannica.com/biography/Rembrandt-van-Rijn.

Books

Cesar, Stanley. *Twenty-Four Rembrandt's Paintings (Collection) for Kids*. Seattle: Amazon Digital Services, 2013.

Krull, Kathleen, and Kathryn Hewitt. *Lives of the Artists: Masterpieces, Messes (and What the Neighbors Thought)*. New York: HarperCollins, 2014.

Spence, David. *Rembrandt (Essential Artists)*. London: Ticktock Books, 2009.

Spremulli, Paul. *Artist Masters for Kids: Rembrandt*. Scotts Valley: Createspace Independent Publishing Platform, 2014.

Venezia, Mike. *Rembrandt (Getting to Know the World's Greatest Artists)*. New York: Children's Press, 2015.

On the Internet

Rembrandt House Museum
http://www.rembrandthuis.nl/

Rembrandt van Rijn
http://www.rembrandtpainting.net/

canal (kuh-NAL)—A manmade ditch that is used to move boats and water from place to place.

canvas (KAN-vus)—Blank fabric on which artists paint.

easel (EE-zul)—A stand or frame that holds an artist's canvas.

etching (ET-ching)—Artwork carved on a hard material, such as wax, that can be used to make multiple prints.

guilder (GIL-der)—A type of money used in the Netherlands until 2002.

masterpiece (MAS-tur-peese)—An especially great piece of created work, such as a painting or sculpture.

musket (MUS-keht)—A long-barreled gun fired from the shoulder.

musketeer (mus-keh-TEER)—A soldier who carries a musket.

parable (PAYR-uh-bul)—A short story that teaches a lesson.

portrait (POR-tret)—A drawing or photo that usually shows just a person's head and shoulders.

printing press (PRIYNT-ing PREHS)—A machine that adds ink onto paper to make copies of text or images.

samaritan (sah-MER-eh-tahn)—A person who helps others.